Never PISS OFF A POET

By Prolific Jones

Prolific Publishing – prolificservices502.info

© Copyright – 2020

All Rights Reserved. No part of this book may be reproduced, stored in a retrieval system, or transmitted by any means without the written permission of the author.

Cover Design: Prolific Jones

ISBN-13: 978-1-951941-24-6

Printed in the United States of America

Acknowledgements

I acknowledge Life.
If I hadn't been blessed with it, I wouldn't have been able to fill the pages of this book with these poems. Although it hurt. But, I wouldn't have been able to feel the hurt if I hadn't have been living and breathing Life right?
I thank anyone that purchased this book because you could have bought someone else's book or decided to do something other than to sit down and read or listen to this book. So once again, " THANK YOU!"

Now, for the disclaimer.

If you are someone that believes that people that love God don't cuss every now and then, Baaaby! This is not the book for you! That would have taken too much time for me to edit. Plus, I wasn't always saved. And to tell the truth, there are days I revert back to the old me, have to repent, and start all over again. If you weren't able to tell by the cover of this book, Honnneyyy! I wrote a lot of these poems when I was pissed!
(Seriously, one of the poems is literally titled ,"Pissed". Hey, it was better than getting locked up)But I'm sure you're not one of those people because you chose to read a book entitled, "Never Piss Off A Poet."

I hope you enjoy. Be Blessed,

Prolific Jones

Table of Contents

Acknowledgements	iii
Never Piss Off A Poet	1
WAR	2
Playing House	4
THE DECADE LONG MISTAKE	5
Silent Reminder	6
Lost Case	8
The Same Old Meaning	10
Dear Little Girl	11
Know My Name	12
Cousins	14
Dear White People	15
Cute Ain't Comfortable	16
Silent Conversation	18

Lift Every Voice	19
I Got Tired Part 1	21
Your Last Chance	23
I Got Tired Part 2	25
Your Wish That Never Came True	26
Psychological	28
Regifted	30
Dream Catchers & Back Stabbers	32
Entrepreneur @ A Interview	34
This Land	36
Pissed	42
Word Play 1.	43
Word Play 2.	44
Weeping	46
Church Hurt	48
The Faith of Ms. Celie	49

Suicide Note	**50**
Changing Places	**51**
Sibling Rivalry	**52**
My Apologies	**54**
Block That Number	**55**
Black Panther Anger	**57**
Those Hats	**59**
Daddy's Girl	**60**
You Tried It	**63**
I'm That Sub	**65**
Dear Master…...I Mean Manager	**68**
When You Love Your Child But Don't Like Them	**71**
Family Ties Broken	**73**
Dr. NSF	**75**
Sounds In The Night	**76**
In Total Agreeance	**78**

Two Confused States Of Mind	80
Free Fall	81
From The Substitute To The Pupil	82
WP Disease	84
Who are you?	89
Nope	90
The Audacity Of Your Stupid Cheating Ass	94
Why Ugly Men Cheat	98
Cheating Man	99
Proverbs From The Old	101
Proverbs Of The Old	102
Sins Forgiven, But Never Forgotten	104
Election	105
How The School To Prison Pipeline Came To Be.	106
S.T.P.P	112

The Bridge Burner & The Under Cover Boss	114
I'm a Thug	115
Can You See?	116
He Doesn't Understand	118
The Phenomenon	119
Sick	121
I Am A Woman	123
I Want A Prolific Experience	124

Never Piss Off A Poet

A Notebook and a Pen are a
poets' most dangerous weapons.
Don't piss me off and then read
my notebook. You may walk away
with feeling lacerated..
The other day, my notebook, my pen, and I
had a long conversation with each other.
And it was all about you.
About why you thought you
could treat people the way you do.
Making promises you never planned to keep.
Ridiculing people that look and act like me.
Smiling in my face and stabbing me
in the back. All at the same time.
Acting as though you are my friend.
Telling everyone you really don't like me.
But at the time, I had the resources you needed
Thinking I was the fool,
but never realizing the joke
Was actually on you.
Never Piss Off A Poet
I Will Ink The Hell Out Of You

WAR

How dare you two?
Now you know that
was just the wrong thing to do.
I, the innocent bystander, came out,
shut my door, and nearly stopped, dropped,
& rolled, all over the floor.
My question is, why'd you have
to double team me though?
Was that your goal?
To catch me while I wasn't
looking and hit me with such intense pain
that I screamed like I was a blond haired
blue eyed California girl, and started wind milling
like I was fighting some chick in
the street all at the same time.
It was so bad, I almost snatched off my
shirt in front of all my neighbors!!!!
Don't think I'm not going to return the favor.
To the store I go.
I ain't dealing with this
no damn mo'! I got my ammunition and
I'm spraying full force.
You and your place of residence are
getting a divorce. Say goodbye
to your momma, your daddy,
your babies, and all your friends.
Yeah you think I'm petty,
but I'm out for revenge.
If you just happen to live through this,

I promise you'll think twice.
I'm coming to take your life.

Playing House

We'd go

looking for houses
then end up

playing house
at my house

on our break
from work.

After work,
he'd go home

and play
house with

his wife and kids.

Then come back

the next day and

start the process

all over again.

THE DECADE LONG MISTAKE

At first, there was a
burning sensation,
but then, a sheet of ice began to form
over what used to be, her heart.
She tossed the phone back
over to his night stand
and began to work on
her agenda for that day.
There had been little
clues throughout the years.
Little hints here and there,
covered up with lies
to keep the truth
from being revealed.
But everything done
in the dark comes to light.
And at 6:30 that morning,
the light began to show itself.
Slowly at first, and then, nothing
could stop it just as,
nothing can stop
the dawn of day, but God.

Silent Reminder

I thought about calling you
and reminding you that it
was your daughter's birthday today.
Then I remembered that 15 years ago,
I called you and told you to be at the hospital
because your baby girl was going to
make her grand entrance into the world.
Although you showed up that day,
you didn't show up for another 14 years.
If you did crawl from under whatever rock
you were hiding under, it was for just
a small moment of time.
Just long enough for her to know
that the man that's
fed her, clothed her,
kept a roof over her head,
wished her happy birthday,
helped me give her birthday parties,
and tucked her in bed all these years,
is not her biological father.
But was the best dad she'd ever had.
Not that I was trying to hide it.
During your hiatuses away out of her life you were an,
"Out of sight, Out of mind," type of situation for me.
And I was just fine with that. So I was okay with you not calling
to wish your daughter happy birthday right up until, our seed
turns to me with hope in her eyes and says,
" Has he called?" Then I turn away
because, I couldn't stand

to see the hope that was emanating
so brightly from her innocent soul
   and respond by saying, "No."

Lost Case

The saddest thing about you,
is that I lowered my standards
and accepted you as you were.
Seeing what you were capable of being.
But sadly, what I saw was only a figment of my imagination
that you don't have the capability of seeing or ever wanting to be.
What's even worse, is that I'm not the only one that has seen the
good in you . But just like me,
they realized, you were a lost cause too.
I know you think that these tears are for
the failed relationship you weren't
capable of being in.
Yes, these tears are for you.
They are for how bad I feel for
your mother, that gave you life,
wasted on carrying you for 9 months.
I feel bad for the fact that she was literally
torn apart while she struggled through
each excruciating contraction
to bring you into this world .
That you have only wasted,
the air God has given you.

Lost Case (Continued)

You are pollution

You are the reason the ozone

layer is disintegrating.

You are the negative in every positive situation.

The sadness I feel for you, can only be deemed as

Pity.

The more I look at you, the more

I get sick to the pit of my stomach.

I regret that I chose to grace your

dark atmosphere with the aura of

my presence. For you

have only blackened

the light I tried to place inside

and around you.

In my life I have learned to call things

for what they are, So to you,

I say," Demon, go back to the pit

in hell you came from. I'm Done."

The Same Old Meaning

I am so tired of people that get
mad if they get called a nigger
calling each other nigga
as if it's a term of endearment.
But still acting like the definition
of a nigger. Doesn't matter if they
live in the worst side of town
or have, "Moved on up". like
the Jefferson's. Or if the color
of their skin is Black, White,
Yellow, Pink, or Brown.
Or if the word ends with
er, uh, or an a.
Any time the letters
n-i-g-g are associated
with any of those
endings that word
still has the
same old meaning.

Dear Little Girl

Dear little girl

in such a big body.

I am going to pretend

that

I fear for

me and my family's

life and call the police

for you instead of

beating the hell out of you.

Like I really want to do.

I guess no one ever

told you that if you

step to adult

you get dealt with

like an adult.

Your Welcome.

Know My Name

You called yourself joking on me in front of your company,
all because you didn't get the attention you felt you needed from me.
Your mistake was not realizing I wasn't always saved.
You've taken my kindness for weakness.
Allow me to introduce you to who I used to be.
I hope you feel better now you, no class having,
need Jenny Craig worse than me,
Body Magic wouldn't even work on you looking mug
You that sloppy ass punk in that commercial
chomping down on pizza while he was at the gym
talking about his new year resolution
was to lose weight.
When I see you coming my way,
I hold my breath 'cause I think you just might stink,
cause you look like you still shit on yourself.
I was giving you a benefit of a doubt before,
but you proved it last night, yo' ass ain't even funny,
you're a Def Comedy Jam wanna be.
You won't ever get anywhere pulling that
shit you tried to pull on me.
Stick with your day job, that is, if you have one.
Take some advice & just stop,
you'll never make it with that garbage.
You think you're funny, but what's funny is that you're the joke.
Now that I've gotten that out, if we ever happen to be
in the same venue or, if we are the last two people
on this earth. I will not even acknowledge that your
shadow is in my presence, don't try to talk to me about my TV

show,
or performing at any of my events, I need someone that can provide true entertainment that won't be at the cost of you ridiculing someone who has paid to attend.
And remember this:
Don't *Ever* Piss Off A Poet
I'm Prolific Jones Bitch!!!

Cousins

He
looks like he could be the
chief of a tribe of Africa.
The other looks like some giant
oompa loompa looking
female finally let Gonzo get some.
And out of that crazy situation,
They had a baby.
But the chief doesn't know who is and allows
oompa loompa & Gonzo's baby to call him
something other than his actual name.
Ironically he calls the chief King Kong.
Attempting to be funny.
But King Kong was the biggest
and baddest around.
I wish I could say him being called
King Kong
was a term of respect
But I can't when I know he's being called
a big black monkey instead.
What's crazy is that they don't realize that
they could be cousins
separated by slavery's hands.

Dear White People

Dear white people
Please realize that not all
black people say the n word.

And that it's not okay to say

not even once much less,

multiple times in our presence

just because of the color of our skin

or how many of us you think

you're cool with.

I don't care you are using it

by the definition given by Webster.

Doesn't matter if the song you are

singing in Karaoke has it in the lyrics.

Mute it out of your mind *and* your mouth.

Just like it does on the screen, and like

you don't event hear it.

Honoring this directive

will keep you alive, unharmed,

and everybody happy.

Signed, Aggravated

Cute Ain't Comfortable

These shoes,
These shoes,
These shoes.
They are so fly!
When I put them on, I go from
Five foot two, to 6 feet high.
I look like I have muscles in
my calves AND in my thighs.
While I'm walking my backside does the
"Shake, Shake, Shake,
Shake, Shake, Shake,"
And the, " Bow Chicka Wow Wow,"
all at the same time.
But while I am walking, looking so fresh and clean.
There's this scream building inside of me.
I realize the scream it's not coming from inside my
chest, but from my feet instead.
When I look around, there are no seats in sight.
If I keep standing here, there's going to be a fight.
It will be between my feet, these shoes,
and the floor. I'm thinking,"
Jesus, just help me make it to the door!!!"
It was 12:04 and now it's 12:09.
It's way past time to sit down
and let my toes unwind, or rather uncurl.
Finally, I see the light!!!
I find a seat waiting just for me!!!
Oh no!! Someone's heading towards my seat of rest!

Lord GOD!!!!! This has GOT to be a test!!!
So I grit my teeth, start running, and take a leap!!!
You better know, that I slid right into that seat!!!
You know you don't mess with a woman
with hurting feet!!!

Silent Conversation

You were wrong. He was wrong
But why oh why did you go around
that corner out of the view of others?
You had to know it was going to happen.
Had to have an inkling of a feeling that if
you kept following behind that man and saying
what you said, there was a chance you might
wind up dead. To tell the truth, I'm surprised
that you're still alive. Why didn't you use that
phone you are now holding in your hand
BEFORE going after that man?
That man you were going after has a name
Although, I don't know what it is,
but this I know this for sure.
HIS NAME IS NOT
nigger

Written May 2020

Lift Every Voice

The problem is that most of us
won't lift our voices and sing anymore.

And for those of us that do, we have
our voices drowned out by the
moans and groans of negativity
heard from this world we now live in.

Allowing our youth to believe
that slavery is truly abolished
and falling through that loop hole
in the 13th Amendment that
is so plain to see, but what's
the point of being able to see
if they can't even read?

That loop hole is a version
of the rope that was used to
lynch our people with.
When it's pulled our people
are snatched and are hanging midair
trying unsuccessfully, to breath.

Lift Every Voice and sing
the stories of our people and
how we have overcome
all that has come before us.

Lift Every Voice and Sing
our songs of Hope and Survival
that course through our veins
and beats within our hearts.

Lift Every Voice and Sing.

I Got Tired Part I

I got tired of asking you to do the things
you promised you would do.
Matter of fact, it really wasn't what you said you
would do. It was what was insinuated when you
laid down and made this baby with me.
I mean who wouldn't expect a father to help with
daily needs to raise a child? Was I wrong to expect you
to be there when our baby was pulled from my womb?
I got tired of asking you to help me with some diapers
and get a few outfits from the dollar store.
Diapers turned into underwear and those onesies
she looked so cute in, turned into bras.
I got tired of ripping up your clothes and layering
them with the dirty diapers you never help purchase and
using my ink to type up your," Till you do right by me and
my baby, this is what you have to deal with," letters in red.
I got tired of you telling me that I owe you money for ripping up your
clothes although you never paid for the shoes I bought to cover our
baby's toes. I got tired of the lame ass excuses you gave me
explaining why
we would never see you for months at a time. You told me you didn't
have money on your books to get some pen and some paper to let me
know you have been locked up one more time.
I got tired of *you*. Then you had the nerve to tell me that your
momma said that I was the best thing that ever happened to you and
you never knew what I would say if you asked me to come back to
you.
Negroid, you already knew what I would say!
So I didn't say not one got' damn thing!
Because I was tired of talking to you.

Giving you chance after chance to be a man.
I got so tired you know what I did one day?
I got her another father and now she calls him daddy.
Now the only time you can look at her face
is on a friend of a friends Facebook page.

Signed,
The Best Baby Momma You Ever Had.

Your Last Chance

She's at her dad's house....
It has taken me 14 years
to be able to say that phrase.
And be speaking about the biological
person that told me he loved me,
ejaculated enough sperm inside me
to birth a tribe, and then, left..
Crazy that you would treat the
product of your own seed worse
than your biological treated you.

You were given the chance to be adopted..
The futile attempt you gave to
act as though you cared about our child almost
kept her from having a real father in her life.
But, believe it or not this is not a
poem I'm writing to bash you.

I have taken my hands off of the situation
and decided to eradicate the hate
I've had for you all these years.
Now I can scratch you off the list
as one of the reasons I may
have ended up going to hell.

It is now up to you to decide whether
or not you are going to be a father or
the invisible entity you've been all these years.
Do me and you both a favor and don't fuck it up.

Sincerely,
The Best Baby Momma
You Ever Had

I Got Tired Part II

I got tired
Your daughter got tired.
My momma got tired.
Your momma got tired
And with my daddy?
You never stood a chance.
We all got tired of waiting
on you to fulfill promises you
never intended on keeping.
You would have been better off just telling us the things
you knew you were never going to do.
Like buying
food, clothes, keeping a roof over
our heads, and being anything but being
the dust storm that pops up every now and again.
Of which you have done time and time again.
How can you tell a child that she is lacking something
you are never able or willing to give?
But I digress. Just wanted to say
Happy Sperm Donor's Day
to the person the person that had
all the opportunity in the world
to become a father but turned into a
Dead Beat Dad instead.
Signed
The Woman That Is
Still The Best Baby
Momma You Ever Had

Your Wish That Never Came True

You have wanted to get with me for so long,
that every time you have been in my presence,
you hire a prostitute so that you can call
them by my name. Because I have turned
you down yet again.

But you know that I know that
being with someone who will let you
call them by my name doesn't come close
to being with me. I am the one and only.

And I hope you realize that I know you are
just one of those people that uses lyrics to
pick up unsuspecting females that are elated
that you have "chosen" them as the one you
will spit your poetic lies to for just one night.

I refuse to be one of your poetic escapades.
You can miss me with that ish...
You should have been a man, when you
stepped to me in the first place

Instead of a pimple faced horny teen that thought
I was going to be his pornographic fantasy.
I love your talent but I hate your ways.
Grow the hell up and get out my face.

Signed,

Your Wish That Will Never Come True.

Psychological

I don't love you.

you were just the way to get out of

the abusive situation I was in when I met you.

But Now but now that I've been with you for so many years,

It's your type of abuse that I've become accustomed to.

The more I grew up the more you reverted to being a kid.

Yes, you supported me when I was going to school

but that wasn't just for me it was for me, and you too

not so you can continue to get fired

and laid off from job after job after job

and become the oldest actor on the,

"Never going to amount to nothing," show.

While I'm slaving to pay the bills on my aching feet

Nor did I go to school to learn a trade so that you can stay at home

and teach our son how to be nothing but be a video game player.

Now please listen to what I'm going to say….

your unemployment or SSI checks do not pay the bills!!

You talk about my family because

we don't have degrees but it was my family that kept

the kids when you went out to sale your little CD.

With your family is always some type of fee.

I know your mother graduated from college

what did she get, a check cashing degree?

Psychological (Continued).

That's why we had to get separate accounts.
Your momma was making my account bounce
more than the birthday bouncy house
the both of you never helped me pay for.
My family will clean toilets just make sure
we meet all of our families needs.
Unlike you who said,
" Custodial or any manual labor
is beneath me, I have a college degree!"
You are the example of the nothing assed
nucka Erika Badu was talking about in
her song. But most of your friends are
worthless too so you can't even call Tyrone.
For the ones who are worthwhile,
You being their friend is past tense.
They grew up and now, they have some sense.
their grown and have their own families to raise
And now you say you're going to get a psychology degree.
God please help me!!! Now you're telling me that I'm
the one that's crazy I guess I am after all the times
you cheated on me. And I listened to you tell
me all the things that I could never be.
But I guess I'm glad you did because it was
you who stirred the rage
hidden inside of me.

Regifted

So that we can make sure we are
completely clear on what's happening here,
You have not won this war. I just chose not to fight.
You are still the woman that had
to sneak to sleep with my husband.
Had to wait and see if I was
in the vicinity before you
could even say hi.
And when you were together,
you were in the shadows never able to
"walk into the light Carol Ann" to show off "*your*" man.

Sometimes the truth hurts, but tonight, it's needed.
You really believe that have finally won what you always wanted.
Somebody else's man you can finally call your own.
Please know that what you are showing
off as a trophy, are my leftovers.
You are the complete opposite of me.
From the color of our skin to
the power we hold within.
My power comes off the
Richter scale, while yours,
doesn't even make a bleep.
You accept whatever he does,
whereas, I, have standards that
he must uphold.

Regifted (Continued)

While you, have this "Yes Dear",
mentality where everything
he says goes. You know how I know?
I know because of the way you run your mouth.
Ever since he let you out the bag, the closet,
or whatever the hell you've been in throughout
the years, it's been running nonstop.
I know, I know, you want to scream,
I FINALLY got my man!
From the snowcapped mountain top.
(Side note: Of which he's not going to climb
with you because he's scared of heights.
I guess you'll have to do it from the
front lawn of YOUR house
he's moving into with you.)
But how do you claim something
that was never yours?
Oh I know! Let's use the
regifting system!
Merry X-Mas to the Side Piece!
She finally got her man!
Along with all the reasons
I didn't want him anymore.
From the woman,
he's still thinks about.
His Wife.
Enjoy!

Dream Catchers & Back Stabbers

I stand looking at myself in the mirror
trying to decide what color of lipstick to wear.
It's hard to decide because I realize
that no matter what shade I choose,
I know I'm still going to be at war.
Red may alert someone that I'm ready to
go head to head with them.
Pink means that I'm letting go
of what was stolen from me and all is forgiven.
& Yellow means I'm scared what people will
think of me once I tell everyone what was done.
But then my eyes land on a metallic burnt orange.
A mixture of the red & pink and
a little gold mixed in between
This color says that although
I've let it go for now
I'm preparing for war at another time.
And I will come out of it shining in the end.
But after I sat back & thought about it,
I decided to wear clear,
so my thoughts & ideas would
be invisible to the eyes that want to see.

Dream Catchers & Back Stabbers (Continued)

You have to be careful who you tell
your thoughts, your plans, or your dreams to.
Its crazy, but some people
don't have enough ambition to
create innovative things on their own.

Instead, they kidnap another's when
they hear someone else's plan or
are invited to participate in
someone's dream becoming
a reality.
Taking the idea as their own.
Never admitting to anyone
where the original plan
came from.

Entrepreneur @ A Interview

Just so we are clear, if you didn't know it before, I am using you.
I am using you for your money. Yeah, I Know you think that I'm
happy for the chance to be part of your crew.
But being part of them and around you just won't do.
I have dreams and
aspirations to pursue.
And you don't even have a clue.
Every little cent that you give me
I am stacking to build the foundation
for my empire I will have when
I finally no longer need you.
All the things I go through while I'm
with you, will add to my experiences
I will use to help my plan come into view.
So yes, I will follow your rules
and do the things you want me to do.
When my kids are sick I won't take them to the doctor.
And I will wait till I've worked 180 days plus overtime before
I ask to go on vacation. I'll wear the clothes you want
me to wear and wont color my hair. I will go to lunch only when
you say I can and if I have a question or need to go to the restroom
I will raise my hand. All this I will do for a while so I can get your
money that
even you have to admit isn't enough to have a decent living.
But I will take it for now. Just until I can take everything
that I need from you. And let's be all the way real about this
you know you're just using me too.
Saw my skills and wanted to use them as your own.
Just know that one day, I'll be gone.

Signed, the Entrepreneur on an Interview

This Land

To my child that whose wide eyed innocence
has gotten you in a mess over this stolen land we live in.
I am not going to try to convince you to believe what I believe.
Because of my age I have had more experiences, have seen more
things that have caused me to think opposite of your beliefs.
Whether you want believe it or not, although I don't doubt your
family has had a rough time. It wasn't because there wasn't an
opportunity to use privilege that was given to your mother.
All due to her skin color.

But she decided to love someone with skin like mine and bring
forth beautiful children that the America you are so determined to
defend, looks down on with distaste and hate.

Just to let you know so that you won't be able to say
that you were never told. If we were in the original days of
slavery, if you and your mother hadn't been killed while she was
still carrying you in her womb, You would have been a pet in your
slave owner's house with a rope tied around your neck.
For their child to hold on to as they dragged and pulled you
around from one place to another. You probably wouldn't
have been no more than the age of two.
You wouldn't have been able to eat at the table or sit the family,
because of you being the pet. So you would be told to eat their

scraps they would throw to you on the floor. That is, if you were even allowed to be in the same room. At night when it was time for everyone to go to sleep, the only way you could sleep in a bed is if you were laying across the bottom of the bed warming the master's, his wife's, or their children's, feet.

This Land (Continued)

While you lay on top of their feet keeping them warm., you yourself would be freezing. For you to have a blanket they would see no need.

After wife's and the children's feet were warm and they had gone to sleep,

you would have to go to another room in the house were the master you would have to meet. Where he would begin to play with you too.

For although you were his child's toy during the day. You'd be the master's toy at night. It wouldn't matter if you were a girl or a boy. Making your slave owners happy is your world. The whole time he's having his fun with you he'd be calling you his beautiful slave nigger girl. Over and over again. Till after so many years of this way of life you would except that that's what you were. Never questioning if you could possibly be anything more. After all you would only be the age of 8, 9, or 10 that's what you are there for. Eventually, the master's wife gets jealous and tells him there is no longer a use for you in the big house anymore and to put you to work in the fields to pick cotton and live in a shack with nothing but a dirt floor. The first day in the field, you get whipped for working to slow. Your skin is ripped apart where the lash hits and you experience pain that you've never had. You want to die the pain is so bad. Throughout the days the pain subsides you learn to

get quicker so that feel the lash of the whip. But then a few months later you have a feeling inside your belly, and the mammy in the quarters says that you are going to have a baby. You begin to cry because you know this child you hold in your womb is no one's but the slave owners. Months later you are in your shack. Holding your beautiful baby daughter, telling her how much you lover her. The birth sack and blood has just been washed off.
She is pink, pretty, and has a head full of hair.

This Land (Continued)

You begin to scream and cry when you look up and see that slave owner has come to the shack to take her.

Telling you that," You gonna have more nigga babies later.

That for this baby people will pay. This color of nigga is the new house slave.

That's when you find out you've gotten a promotion.

You are now the one of the birthing niggas for the whole plantation.

A few years and multiple babies later, your owners cousins come to visit and you see a beautiful little girl with a rope around her neck being pulled to in and fro in front of the plantation. You stare with dread and tears start to form. The little slave girl looks at you with eyes

JUST…. LIKE…. YOURS

This is the America you are defending. But will America defend you?

Be careful for they are trying to bring back Slavery, Segregation, & abolish Civil Rights for us all. Trying to go back to the way this country began on land that never belonged to them..

But because you've defended America so well,

they might just make you the new

birthing slave for Kentucky State.

06-01-2020

I wrote this poem so many years ago. And today my city
is in the middle of Protests, Riots, Looting, and
looks like we're in the middle of a war.
Because the police have again,
killed another African American Soul.

Pissed

I am trying my best to
forgive and forget.
But it's very hard for me to do.
Because of my religion I know
that's what I'm supposed to do.
But my religion, has a book that
has a verse that says an eye for an eye.
That where I'm confused.
Because although I was raised to do
what's "right", I want to beat your ass too.
I'm trying my best to do everything the
"civilized way" but truthfully, I just want to go
back to who I was back in the day.
Because I wasn't always saved.
I am sick of everyone thinking I'm
so nice and sweet that the shit they do
to me and mine won't cause they asses to get beat.
Or Cut, Or Ran Over then backed up on,
and run over again, until
I am sure you know
that I am pissed off at you.

Word Play

1.

Size doesn't
matter to me
it's the taste
I'm worried about
you see. Skinny,
medium sized,
fat, or fat @ the
top and then
skinny at the
bottom, they are
all delicious to me.
and the sauce it just
makes it better, sweet
and sticky, a little
salty and thick.
I *love* all of them
no matter the size.
I love me some
Chicken
Fingers
and
Fries!

Word Play

2.
Yesterday,
I paid
a woman
to pleasure my
husband
while I watched.
Heard him as
he moaned and
sighed in enjoyment
Saw his eyes dilate
and his back arch
when she touched
him in all the
right spots.
He came
and apologized
to me afterwards.

I told him
don't worry about
it baby.
I'm not mad at all.

you needed
that pedicure
much worse than me.

Weeping

Small, tiny tracks of sorrow keep falling from my eyes
and down my face. Without me making a single sound.
I try to act like everything's ok. But these silent tears are
giving my feelings away. The things that have happened
to people I don't even know are keeping me under the
covers in my bedroom. I am silently weeping for the people
that have skin like me, no longer being able to breathe.
Houses being rammed. One shot being fired from
one side, trying to protect life, the other multiple shots
needlessly taking life in the middle of the night.
All of this taking place
In   The   Wrong   House.
Arms that could have been my husband's handcuffed
for, **"Protecting While Being Black"**.
In spite of the uniforms in blue being the ones that attacked.
The hero is still breathing but was sent to jail because he
knew that their, "Black Lives Mattered."
Film being taken of yet another knee in the neck of
another man with brown skin unsuccessfully trying to
Catch   His   Breath
Screaming Momma as he goes into an eternal sleep.
Having the police called for being
"Black While Bird Watching"
Blatantly being lied on
Because he asked
White Privilege to put a leash on.
Then wake up to read about two little girls
Being shot in the park.
All of this along with over 100,000 getting sick.

I guess I'm weeping because my soul knows
that it's only Going To Get Worse

I'm done.
I'm trying life tomorrow.

Church Hurt

It's a wonder that I still call myself a Christian.
If you go by all the times that I've been hurt by
"Christians" or hurt people myself while calling
myself a Christian is amazing.
I could literally wear a shirt with church
steeples and a bunny hopping to each one for
all the times that I have "Church Hopped"
every time either of these situations have happened.
From being touched by family and friends
that were supposed to be Christians.
From sleeping with the deacon,
and him marrying my cousin.
To the Holy Ghost filled sisters at the church telling me
that I was wearing my clothes to tight and short
in order to entice the preachers and deacons while
directing the choir. But never once asking if there was
anything I was needing.
To being told that my baby wasn't a blessing from
God because I wasn't married at my baby shower
by a preacher of the word.
To loving the minister of music
who was already married.
To trying to do what Jesus would do and
willingly help someone who is so holy and has
been in church all their life, even though they
reeked havoc on my family's lives.
It truly is a wonder that I call myself a Christian at all.
Just those situations alone would be enough to
make you ask," Why even answer the call?"

The Faith of Ms. Celie

All them years Mister was beating the hell out
of Celie, he was tearing down the empire that
they could have built together.
Sad that he had to be cursed before he saw
the pot of gold he'd had all along.
Sad that he and Celie's step father would treat
any woman the way she was treated.
Sad to have the children that were molded
in your womb snatched from your arms,
barely given the chance to inhale their scent.
Sad to be beaten and raped by a man
who was supposed to love you as your husband.
But Celie was God's child and everything
the devil took from her was given back to her
in abundance. Yes, there were tears and there
was doubt at times that she was anything other than
a child of God, because of everything she endured.
But Ms. Celie never lost her faith.
Now I encourage you to look at everything
your going through and know there's a reason for
all that is happening to you and try having
just a mustard seed of Ms. Celie's faith.

Suicide Note

Tap tap tap tap.
Silence.
Delete. Tab over.
Tap tap tap enter save.
Save, I wish someone could save me
from what I'm about to do to myself.
But if I don't people will say I'm not normal,
because I'm not like them. To be honest,
I don't even desire to be like them one bit.
So I guess there has to be something
wrong with me. So I save this document
and start sending it out. I want it to be
seen early in the day, so that by the
afternoon, the deed will have been done.
My light will be extinguished. I will cease
to exist as the person I've been known to be.
That's what turning in this resume and
getting a job is doing to me.

Changing Places

There was a time when Black Men

protected their women and children.

Those days are now like drops

of dew that evaporate into air.

Still there but invisible to the eye.

Now women have learned that

they have to put on the pants

even though they'd much

rather be wearing the dress instead.

Sibling Rivalry

Sometimes the most beautiful people on the outside
have the ugliest personalities on the inside.
If you were as beautiful on inside as you were
on the outside you would be a happier person.
I would tell you to treat people the way you
want to be treated but it seems as though
you don't believe you deserve to be treated
any better. I can tell by how mean
and evil you treat people.
I believe you have literally cursed yourself
by treating your own sister the way you do.
And not only do you do this yourself,
but you try to get others to treat her the same as you do.
Alienating her, and trying to get people to think
she is the crazy one. When in all actuality, it's you.
You are the one that's crazy. The jealousy and hate
you have for your sister has made you so miserable that
you will do anything to make your sister look bad.
But I am on the outside looking in and I can see that you
are hurting too. You are hurt because she has the things
you can't have, and she has reacts to what you do,
because hurt people, hurt people. Until you begin to love yourself
you will never truly be able to love another person.
Maybe that's why you have never been able to have the thing you
have wanted the most. God is giving you time to learn to love
yourself as He loves you. Start loving yourself then you will begin
to s
how love to others, and when God believes you are
ready you will have the desires of your heart.

It's a sin to hate. But people sin every day.
Because we are human. Stop hating your sister.
Or else, one day, you won't
have that sister around that you've hated for so long.
You will be miserable and left all alone.

My Apologies

Dear Ancestors from near and far.

With deep regret, I come to report that status of the

youth of your generations.

I am so sorry to say that

although so many of you were beat, spit on,

hung from trees, & died for your future

generations to be treated like human beings

they don't care about the things you did

that gave them their rights.

Instead, they act like simple minded fools and thugs.

The majority of them are disrespectful to their elders,

teachers, and themselves.

I hope the prayers you prayed, the life you led

with hope and every step you

took while marching for our rights are still covering us,

and were not in vain.

Block That Number

I don't know why but, this Crackhead, keeps trying
to contact me. They sent a text one night AND
tried to call me all in one night. My husband looked
at me and said". Baby, Do me a favor,

BLOCK.............THAT......... .NUMBER."

I replied with," Yes, Harpo." And immediately
complied with my husband's directive.
THEN! This fool tried to friend me on the book
of face and in boxed me too!
I don't know what he thought sending me a
message that read, "Call me baby mamma" would do.
I stopped being his "Baby Momma" when I married
a real man who adopted my baby when she was four.
Had a letter signed, sealed, and delivered, that said
my baby, was no longer yours.
So whatever it is he has to say,
I don't want to hear it. It's probably all
Bullshit and Lies.
Just like it's been all my baby's life.

If he's calling to say he played the lottery and
became a millionaire he can call my 18 year old and
give her some money.

If he called to say he's dying, I wish him well on
becoming fertilizer for the ground.
That will probably be the best thing he has
ever done for this world and somehow,
he'd probably mess that up too.

He needs not call
to say not one miniscule
thing to me.
My daughter is now 18.

Black Panther Anger

I cried tears of frustration as my daughter told me
about her day at work where she was called a black
bitch by a pale faced customer and then told to pick
up money that was dropped on purpose in the drive
thru by yet another pale faced customer. She handled
it much better than I would have by smiling and
saying Thank you and have a nice day anyway.
Today was only her second day.
Needless to say, she is now in search of a new job.
Not because she got fired, but because her Momma is crazy.
#dontmesswithmybaby #racismin2017
#Jesusbeaneletricfence #IpleadthebloodofJesus
#Iwasntalwayssaved

Black Panther II

My daughter has now been called a bitch by grown adult white women twice in her 16 years of life. The first time it was her teacher who said that, she was hoping that the "bitch" situation wouldn't come up. When I asked her why she didn't say anything when she called me to tell me my daughter was acting up and was being disrespectful.

Then turns around and says she didn't say it when a complaint was made.

I need everyone that decides they are going to work in a field with ECE, BD, LD children. Just because a child is learning disabled does not mean that they come from a home that uses foul language. Calling anyone a bitch is not normal. You are not going to gain a relationship with my child my doing anything like that. Lastly, the two women that said this to my child were lucky that I wasn't there when they called my daughter out of her name.

They would have experienced me in rare form.

Those Hats

Those hats are red in symbolism of our blood that has run over the cotton our ancestors were forced to pick, the babies they were forced to birth, the whips that peeled back our ancestor's flesh.
If they were to make them blue it would be a symbol of the water our ancestors drowned in trying to escape the Black Holocaust, slavery.
If they turn it green it would symbolize the land they were forced to nurture, the grass we ran across, and the trees that shielded our ancestors as they ran towards freedom on the Underground Railroad.
If they make it orange it symbolizes the color of the sun in Africa during the most beautiful sunset.
If they make it purple it symbolizes the Royalty they **STOLE** from Africa.
What has failed to be seen is that it doesn't matter what color the hat is. It is the meaning of those words they use. That slogan was used by the KKK in the 1920s to promote white supremacy.

And them saying that people of color or Mexican decent are wearing the hats to doesn't mean a thing.

Those are the people that have allowed themselves to be brainwashed & have chosen not to see what's right in front of their eyes. A Voluntary Blindness is what they are experiencing. They've chosen to be the new Uncle Toms in this, "Land Of The Free".

Daddy's Girl

I love my husband, but the man
I love most in the world is my Daddy.
I am a bonafide straight up Daddy's Girl.
And just like the saying goes, Daddy is always right.
Most of the time. But in this case, he is wrong.
But it's not his fault, because he didn't know.
And you can't know what you don't know.
I am the one that went to church, never did drugs,
didn't drink that much, and barely even cussed.
But the mistakes I made are so huge they
gave me Goliath sized skeletons that can
barely be stuffed in my closets.
Especially when you can't forgive yourself
and have family, that won't let you forget either.
When it comes to my wayward child, everyone wants to
blame me and who I let my child be around. Saying that it's
because they smoked weed and how they would have NEVER let
me be around people that smoked that mess when I was a child.
And had I not let my child be around those type of people my child
wouldn't be doing the things she's doing now.
I tried to hold this secret it in but had to let it go.
That one of my first babysitter's, the one that kept my hair so neat,
and her house so clean, cleaned so much so she could get rid of the

smell of cigarettes and weed. But all he knows is that when he came in her house, all he ever smelled was the fragrance of bleach.

Daddy's Girl (Continued)

And the family members that everyone thinks
so highly of because they haven't made the mistakes
I made, are drunks and smokes weed all day.
Said he knows that the baby's daddy is mentally retarded.
Like I would have sex with someone like that on purpose.
Even told me he hoped she was someone else's when
the Sperm Donor asked for a paternity test.
There are some people that smoke
crack and recover and then
there are others that never recover.
The Sperm Donor is the latter.
When I met him, he was working a job
took me shopping, helped me pay my bills,
and helped with everyone else's kids.
I got pregnant, that crack smoking
showed its face, and all that changed.
18 years later, Daddy is still saying
I told you so. Guess he'll do that
the rest of my life
He just won't let it go.

You Tried It

Look let me go ahead and put
it all out on the table now.
Because you seem to think that
I need you in order to become what I already am.
Or you have the audacity to think that
you're the one that put me where I am today.
I'm going to fix that fairy tale notion you
got going in ya' head say,

Ya' Didn't.
So stop with all that Broke Back Mountain,
High School Musical, Mean Girls, bull you trying to pull. Get
some Business Man Etiquette about your ass and Grow The Hell
Up. Stop Calling, Texting , & Threatening my business, saying that
ain't nobody
gonna do nothing to you cause you the HNIC.
When in all reality yo' ass
is just an employee.

Get your life and stop trying to live through mine.
You not the first nor will you be
the last to try to make less of me.

I don't know how many other people
you've tried doing this to.
Doesn't matter if
they were married or single fool.

No real woman who knows who

and what they are is going to want a
Messy, Wanna Be, Jealous,
Jangalang Looking Ass Nigga.

I'm *That* Sub

The other day, I had a student who didn't like
my personality and decided that they were going
to hurt my feelings and call me a bitch.
Then I looked at that child and just smiled shocked,
she screams, "What the hell are you smiling about?"
Turning to the rest of the class she says," This bitch is stupid."
She sittin' up here smiling when someone's calling her out of her name."
Well, at that point I start laughing, then the class starts laughing.
But it was a nervous laugh like they didn't know who to laugh at,
the student, or at me which made me laugh even harder.
"Miss Thang" got mad because she soon realized
that the joke was now on her. The laughter died
down and this is what I said to the wannabe
class clown with a smile on my face.
I say, "I'm not stupid, but I am crazy.
When I say crazy I mean one pink pill short of
a check crazy." She looks at me with confusion
in her eyes and I say," I can tell you didn't think
a person who talks like they have sense could be crazy
or maybe you thought because I have clothes and shoes on,
my hair is done and my face is beat to the ***gods***,
that I can't be crazy. That I am just this boring teacher
that knows nothing about living a hard life when
in all actuality, I do. Sometimes the people that look
like they have it all together on the outside are the
ones screaming from within.
By age 8 I learned how to deal being rubbed
and touched on by the female or male

babysitter that moonlighted as a molester.

By the time I was 14, I had gotten used to being called a bitch, a slut, and a whore along with being bit, spit on, choked, smothered, and beat on all by my own mother.

I'm *That* Sub (Continued)

So when you call me out of my name, it doesn't
bother me it proves that you don't feel good about
yourself .That you don't think you are intelligent
enough to speak positivity into your atmosphere.
That you have to be the negative person you are
because no one ever told you:
How beautiful you are
That you are capable of greatness,
That you can be anything you want to be.
And that you, my dear come from royalty.
What bothers me the most is that I am
realizing that someone may have
hurt you like all the people
that hurt me, and that although
I'm not your blood,
I am sorry that
I wasn't able to protect you.
I'm sorry that no one tried to help you.
But I'm here now so if
you ever feel the need to talk to
me you can. There's a lot you'd be
surprised that I understand.
If you don't want to talk
and would rather write, that's alright.
Sometimes you have to write
out your thoughts
in order to issues to light.

Dear Master…....I Mean Manager

I would rather work 24\7 for myself to build my empire, than work 8 hours a day for you and make the pennies you think you are being gracious enough to give me.
As if making your life richer should be my only objective in life. Forget that I have kids to raise and my own dreams to pursue. What is my making you rich and accepting your pennies gonna do for us?
Nothing but teach us to assimilate into a slavery like society we will grow to hate. The chains and the whips are no longer physical. The slavery game is now mental.
But this game still have the same outcome.
If you don't think I'm working hard or fast enough, I am punished by a write up, a pink slip, or fired.
When I interviewed you saw the royalty in me and decided to hire me so that you could take the light of my royalty out of me. No matter how hard I tried to fight it, my royalty slowly dwindles away. Replaced with the need for that paycheck every other Friday.
Till the point that it's a low glow and then, "Poof," it's gone. So No , Master, I Mean Manager.
You will never hear me say.
I just LOVE, this job you gave me that only pays me minimum wage that doesn't begin to pay me for all the work I do for you. Just as long as your happy with the money you make." Or,
"Yes Master, I mean Manager,
I LOVE this job where you are given the right to tell me when I can go to the bathroom and can take a lunch break."

Or Yes Master, I mean Manager.
I LOVE this job that tells me that my
job duties are more important than
religion and my family members

Dear Master……..I Mean Manager

Making you richer while I become
poorer, is my first priority.
Ironically, when I try to get any type of temporary
assistance, I'm told I make to much money to get or
enroll in the training programs that I could learn the
skills and get loans needed to run my own business.
All because of the pennies you give me.
This is said to me when I can barely keep the
lights on and I barely have enough food for
my kids to eat. All because I have assimilated to
your system where I am working my hardest to
get that 60 cent raise you promised me
I could get if I worked 6 months.

But compared to all the hard work I did in those
6 months for that 60 cent raise was just pennies compared
to the thousands of 50 and 100 dollar bills I've put in
your register. I wanted to go to school but financial aide
is out too because of the pennies you give me yet again.
So I would still have to work for you
So when you ask me, do I like my job, I tell you,
"It's my *Season* to work this job,
it's not my *Purpose*."
And you respond with, "You are going to be one of
my longest workers because you said that."
I say, Thank You. You just made
light of royalty begin to shimmer

My "Season," was over a month later.

When You Love Your Child But Don't Like Them

Still dealing with this mess.
Because she has never been a ward of the state,
she can't be legally emancipated, beyond control warrants won't help
because the system is over run with kids that are wards of the state,
mental health facility discharged her after a few weeks, KY
Challenge is a challenge for us and says she has to make the choice
to come there, I can't force her, School Counselor tells CPS we
abused her when she was disciplined. Now we have a investigation case.
Safe Place calls their spot a vacation away from
the parents, and she can walk out whenever she wants.
Tried counseling, and now she thinks her telling us her "feelings"
in this disrespectful tone she talks to us in is okay and
swears that she isn't being disrespectful when
told that she's being disrespectful and rude.
She says no one but her father and I have a problem
with the way she talks. That we need to accept the way she
is cause she tired of acting the way that I have raised
her cause that's not her. That respect goes both ways.
But how can you respect someone that goes out of
their way to disrespect you virtually every day?
If we discipline her the way she deserves we get a case
and CPS comes to investigate.
I'm told if we leave her at the Home of the Innocents,
we could have neglect charges placed on us.
Since she is almost 18 no one's going to do anything.
But wait for her to turn 18 and lock her up.

When You Love Your Child But Don't Like Them (Continued)

I am fighting so hard for her not to be,
part of this plan white Amerikka has devised to
lock up or kill my baby. But what can I do when she
tries her best to make the stereotype about black people
true? She acts like I'm the enemy and she hates me.
It pisses me off when I vent about this crap we are
going through and people say,
"She's just going through a phase."
"She's just spoiled." or
"You used to do the same
thing when you were her age."
This shit she's doing is not a phase,
it's a lifestyle. She's not spoiled.
She has life messed up! If I did the crap she's
done to us, to *my* parents, she wouldn't be here.
Because I would have been laying in my grave a long
time ago. This child was told no on a regular because
I couldn't afford the majority of the stuff she asked for.
And since she started pulling this bull smiggady we do
only what we have to, keep a roof over her head and food
in her mouth. If she were anyone but my child
treating me like this, they would have been
cut from my life 5 years ago.
When this mess first began.
But she is my child. I have
to figure how we can get
through this without
knocking her ass out.

Family Ties Broken

Lies are spoken choices that will cause family

that once loved each other to look at each other with hate.

Families allow Jealousy and Money to break them apart.

Not speaking for years over a hardened heart.

People of blood relation being accustomed to

being on the outside always looking in

It's sad to see a family with such potential

to be great, be broken apart.

The illusion of a family working together

Gives the black sheep and the misfits

a small spark of hope that things will get better.

But the spark is extinguished when the

candle to the flame is taken away.

Proving that nothing ever changed,
Things are still the same.

Family Ties Broken (Continued)

Lies are spoken choices that will cause family

that once loved each other to look at each other with hate.

Families allow Jealousy and Money to break them apart.

Not speaking for years over a hardened heart.

People of blood relation being accustomed to

being on the outside always looking in

It's sad to see a family with such potential

to be great, be broken apart.

The illusion of a family working together

gives the black sheep and the misfits

a small spark of hope that things will get better.

But the spark is extinguished when the

candle to the flame is taken away.

Proving that nothing ever changed,
Things are still the same.

Dr. NSF

I feel like I felt when I found
out I had just had a miscarriage.
To find out that at one time,
there was this small chance of hope implanted
inside me. That, At first my body welcomed this piece
of hope with welcome arms and then changing her mind
and ejecting my baby with me having no say so in the matter.
It doesn't matter that I didn't know I was pregnant
(I didn't know they would keep charging my account)
I doesn't matter how much I wanted my baby. (My Money)
Leaving me with an empty womb. (Bank Account)
My baby's light extinguished as soon as I found out that
the essence of my baby was there they're aura was snatched
away from me. Never giving me the chance to find out
if I was holding a King or a Queen within my womb.
I had the knowledge of my check being deposited into my
account but the bank snatched my money away from me before
I got to see what my new balance was. Messing up all
the things I had planned. When you really look at,
The bank raped me. Took what I had and left me to die.
When you realized I was still alive and had just a little

bit of life inside you came back and gave me an unwanted,

involuntary, unneeded, and uncalled for abortion.
All the work I put into birthing money into my

account was for nothing to See, Taste, Touch, or Smell.

All I paid for was a visit from Dr. NSF.

Leaving me with nothing but tears of hurt and frustration

Sounds In The Night

One night a slave owner, Master Matthews and his wife set out on their porch looking their grounds bathed in the moonlight enjoying the sounds they heard in the night air.
They laughed and chuckled at the noises they heard coming from the slaves quarters.
They laughed as they heard the moans and the cries of the newest slaves that were still shackled in chains and the sound of the whip connecting and tearing off the fragile skin of the slave in training.
The slave owner says," Oh Thomas will train them right.
His wife says," John do you think He'll be able to...."
just as the sound of a whip cracks through the air tearing more flesh away from the body of the newest slave along with,"
You niggers are going to learn today!" went through the air.
"Oh yes, Thomas will train them right. He's training them just the way I trained him when he came to this plantation as a new slave when he was age 8.
"Oh good." his wife says breathing a sigh of relief, and continues to look over their land.
Centuries later, old Master Mathews and his wife are still enjoying that laugh for our people are still calling each other nigger, beating, and killing each other just the same way they did during slavery and segregation, despite the marches for freedom and civil rights.
No matter how many times, or Lift Every Voice And Sing And have" We Shall Overcome." Deep in our hearts.
Some of us still act like the slaves that came out of the plantations.
It doesn't matter how you say it regardless if you have been with begin with Nigg and end with ER or if you end with an A.
You are still calling each other niggers.
The ancestors of our slave owners enjoy it either way.
For it proves that they broke a society that was full of royalty down into people that act like animals and mindless beings.
Allowing the slave owners family's to make us their 24 hour comedy show. Striving to please the slave owner and never returning to the

Kings and Queens we were
and are, still capable of being.

In Total Agreeance

His family says that they don't understand
why I'm mad at them and won't let them see MY baby.

That they didn't do anything to me or My baby. And that
it's so sad that they haven't seen her since she was an infant.

And I agree with their sentiments. They are completely right.
They haven't done a damn thing to or FOR us.

They didn't do anything when I asked for help with diapers.

They didn't do anything when I asked you for help with clothes.

They didn't do anything when I asked you for help with food.

And there are many other occasions that they didn't do anything.

And most people would say that was my fault. That a closed mouth
don't get fed. And I'm in total agreeance with that phrase.

But I refused to ask them for anything long before my baby was
the
tender age of 2. For the things they themselves asked me
if MY baby needed, they would never do. The times I would
bring her to their house and they would write down
her newest size. Was simply a way to conversate and pass the time.
Up till she was in her third year of being a teen, the most
they had ever done for her was bought her a bag of skittles and
a bottle of tea. Which is ironic if you think about it
That those two items are symbols of death of a life that
never have the chance to grow again. Just like the
relationship between her biological's family
that will never have a chance because they
never took the time to give love

to what could have been.
They haven't done a damn thing.
Yes, I'm in total agreeance.

Two Confused States Of Mind

The problem in this situation
is that we have two confused states of mind.
The mind set of the one who's only donation
in life to me was his seed.
And the mind set of the product of that seed.
My child, my daughter.
For some reason the contributor believes that
his one time donation to me will cover all
needs from the deposit of his donation 16 years ago,
all the way throughout the rest of my child's life.
And unfortunately this product of the egg, that
traveled through my tubes, met his sperm,
and settled in my womb for 9 months thinks that too .
She thinks the piece of garbage, that helped create
but just met, her 2 years ago is really going to do more for her
than the man that has helped me raise her for the last 8 years.
She is so mad at my helpmate because he is not the
one that contributed to her creation. And the one that was
given the chance to contribute thought he had the right to
say that product of his seed was never at home because on
the days that "he" spoke to her she was at someone else's house.
You piece of shit!
You have no rights!

Free Fall

I am free falling, from the tallest building,
with no parachute to pull me back,
allowing me to float safely to the ground
People that don't believe what I know will
say that I'm crazy for just letting go.
But its not their opinion I should worry
about for it's to God I go.
So I stand on the roof of this building
right at the edge, lift my hands, lean over, and let go,
with my eyes wide open, so I won't miss
a thing that's coming my way.
As I fall, people are looking up and pointing, and
trying to redirect my path, but I can't hear
their silent screams. Which is so ironic because
before, they pretended not to hear or see
how miserable they were making me.
People are going to wonder why I did this to myself,
why I didn't wait and get help.
But people don't believe what it is that I know.
For God is the Creator of this poem I
go through called Life.
I quit my job and became an
entrepreneur today.

From The Substitute To The Pupil

Dear 13 year old student.
The audacity of your racism towards me from you
and your counterparts proves that there is truly
White Privilege.

For you to believe that I, a 40 year-old woman should speak to
you, a 13 year-old child, as my equal is ridiculous!
To do that would open the door to you telling
me what to do in this classroom.

You will never have any of the experiences that I have
dealt with in my lifetime that would cause us to become equals,
child.
I've been teaching classes before you were the size
of a pea inside your momma's belly.

Believe it or not, I am not paid to come into the
classroom and follow your every command,
nor am I paid to be your friend.
I am paid to teach you all that I can in my way,
by following your teacher's lesson plans.

What you are "requesting" of me would be the
beginning of what your ancestors demanded f
rom my people. So excuse me if I

never

see you

as my equal.

WP Disease

Response by a Wide Eyed Innocent about racist cop
in Prospect, KY on a post she says:" *Unfortunately,
there is hate all over. Some hidden and some out in the open....
.all wrong and sad. I do want to bring to the attention of all that
hatred does not just occur against black people. It happens against
ALL people.
There are places in Louisville that I definitely wouldn't
go because I'm 1)white and 2) female.
In 2018 it should NOT be like this ."*
Written March 23, 2018.
My Response that would have had her upset.
So I didn't post.
No it shouldn't be like this in 2018.
But it **NEVER** should have been **LIKE THIS**.
*Black People should have never been enslaved.
*There should have never been whips and nooses
we were terrorized and lynched with.
*There should have never been White and Colored Only Signs.
*Blacks should have never been told to give our seats up for a
white person or seat in the back on a bus.
*There should have never been black churches bombed that
killed so many along with 4 black little girls .
*There should have never been the hundreds if not thousands of
blacks killed and attacked by police brutality.
It should not be, but there is over and over again.
When the media FINALLY admits that a white person is
the one bombing, people know that he was targeting blacks.
But they won't admit that, but talk about how he was brought up in
a

God fearing and loving family.
But when a young black boy who was walking home with a bottle of
tea and a bag of skittles is hunted down and shot by an wannabe cop.
Young decisions he made in his short life would have been looked at as a mistake for a white kid time and time again. But because of his beautiful melanin skin, his decisions are magnified and criminalized.

WP Disease

A Black man holding HIS OWN cell phone in HIS OWN
back hard is shot 20 times.
But a white person who shoots up a theatre of people
is treated to McDonald's.
A Black woman pulled over for an uncalled for traffic stop.
Is pulled out of her car and arrested right on camera and then
found dead hours later in her cell. We still don't know what the
really happened.
What the hell?!!!
Black youth are thrown on the ground with grown knees
digging in their backs and arrested at a swimming party.
A white woman spits on and slaps police officers
multiple times, while cussing them out before getting arrested.
What about the white guy that continuously fought the cops before
getting arrested? Not shot or tased, not beat, not choked, so there
was no reason to say", I -Can't -Breathe,"
He was just arrested.
When Black Lives Matter protestors were peacefully
protesting. They are looked at as criminals and trouble makers for
believing that we matter and that we shouldn't be brutalized and
killed by the police.
When White Sandy Hook kids started protesting gun laws they
were looked at as fearless leaders standing up for their rights.
And let it also be said that the reason you as a white female
wouldn't go to some of these places that you won't go to
Day or Night is most likely because of them being in
predominantly black areas and you are scared.
Although your comment is true, let it be said that if something
were to happen to you because of you being a white female there

would be more of a outcry and more of an investigation done to bring the criminal to justice than there ever would ever be for a black male or female. If you don't know, that is something called White Privilege that is automatically given to you because of the color of your skin.

WP Disease (Continued)

When we as black people are born, our first cries are

translated into screams that say,

" Ashes to Ashes, Dust to Dust. "

Because although we just want to live the life that we have

been blessed with and be successful at,

we have to worry about being unjustly accused

and attacked by people who think just like this racist.

Very few of you will admit to seeing what we see.

White Privilege brainwashes you into really

believing in the comment you just said with wide eyed innocence.

In spite of that, I invite you to take off the rose colored

glasses you are looking through and attempt to see what I see.

But then again you won't, because you've got that WP Disease.

Who are you?

I am the descendent of Kings and Queens,
Philosophers, Astronomers, Scientists,
Historians, Explorers, Doctors, Inventors,
Artists, Dancers, Singers, Poets, & more.
I will walk in the strength of knowing that my
ancestors were people of Immeasurable Intelligence.
As I grow under the covering that my ancestors
have blessed me with, I will tell my children our story.
So that, they can tell their children, and they can tell their
children. of the joys and the pains that our people have
endured to get where we are. So that our story will never be
forgotten and our children will find themselves and never
become lost again. For if you don't know where you come from,
you are a lost soul in a barren land.
Ask me who I am.
And I will say to you.
That I am the descendent
Of the beginning.
I am a descendent of Africa.
and will hold my head high and
look you in the eye while telling you so.

Nope

To the people that are complaining about the
celebration of Black History Month,
the pictures that are in our newsfeeds on
our social media pages, the waving of our Red,
Black, Green, & Yellow Flags.
Or the ones that are saying we need to put the
past so we can all get along.
Although, your people are,
Still making Shirts with nooses on them
and selling them in your stores.
*Still driving around with the Confederate Flag
on your car windows and doors.
* Still call us that "Black girl or Black boy"
when you bring us up in your conversations,
choosing to forget that we have a name.
* And wearing your "maga" hats.
(We know your version of making America great
means Black people being your slave again.
That is straight bullshit & you and, especially I, know it.
The only way to try to keep history from repeating
itself is to learn from the tragedies of past.
There are 60, 70, 80, & 90 year old elders that still cry
at the thought of the atrocities that were done to them,
their parents, grandparents and ancestors during
the time of the Black Holocaust and other events
in what you call this great country.
There are museums that get funded millions, if not
trillions of dollars in remembrance of what happened to
white families in Germany 365 days of the year.

But when it comes to celebrating
Black History Month, it's a problem for you.
Even though it's the shortest month of the year.

Nope (Continued)

We give reverence to Our ancestors,
*Our Queens who were raped & forced to be
birthing machines for the plantations.
*Our Kings who were also raped and were also forced
to make babies with WHOEVER they were told to impregnate.
*Our ancestors who were forced to work in the heat of the
summer and the snow of the winter. Picking cotton
by hand that pricked their fingers .
*Our ancestors that had their children ripped for their
wombs after holding them so close to their hearts for 9 months.
*Our ancestors that fed their owners children from
their own breasts.
*Our ancestors that were beat, hung, spit on, choked, and shot by
slave owner, & then the Ku Klux Klan that turned in their uniforms
of white for uniforms dyed in blue, simply because of the color of
their skin.
*Our ancestors who invented the majority of the things used today
that rarely get the credit for it because it was given to or taken by
white people.
*Our ancestors that were not allowed to
drink from the whites only water fountains,
*Or use the whites only restrooms,
*Or eat in the whites only restaurants,
*Or shop in the whites only stores
*Or go to the whites only schools.
Our Ancestors,
Our Family,
Our People
DESERVE to be remembered & celebrated too!

Or do you have the audacity to think that this
is something only white people can do?

The Audacity Of Your Stupid Cheating Ass.

For two and a half years, I suffered through the
stupidity and the ridicule of being with you.
Believing that I could "Help" you and change
you into the man I needed you to be for me
But what I didn't realize was that you were looking
for the mother that deserted you, in me and every
other woman you cheated on me with.
And then, we made the insane decision to make a baby.
And went to work on that decision with fervor and haste.
The more we worked, the stupider you became.
By the time I admitted how stupid you were,
it was time to give our baby her name.
I went to the doctor to get a shot and a brown paper bag.
But came home with a due date and a W.I.C appt. instead.
I called your friend's cell to tell you the news because you
had no phone of your own. Then this fool told you to tell me that
you had to see the papers before you believed I was having your
baby.
Now that friend has the audacity to be a preacher!! But I digress.
So off to the doctor we went. Your shirt in my fist.
Then you had the audacity to think you were going to sit
in the waiting room in spite of all the times you climbed
in my window and slid between my sheets.
You were snatched up in front of everyone in the office
so you could see the product of your seed on the big screen.
After our baby's first on screen premier, you disappeared.
then reappeared at my door when I was in month 4.
Had the audacity to get upset because my new man greeted

you at the door the day of your "miraculous" appearance.
You thought that I was going to be the lonely pregnant
chick waiting on you to come Ha!!!!
Now that makes me laugh thinking of the audacity of that!!!
Talking about you had been locked up and had nothing on your books for
pen and paper in order to prove you weren't being a dead beat father.

The Audacity Of Your Stupid Cheating Ass (Continued)

You didn't have the decency to get out of the car
and check on me when I fell during the audacity of you
arguing with me. I guess you looking out the rear view mirror
as you drove off was supposed to be your version of you proving
that you were a good father.
Fast forward five more months that you weren't around.
To the night before our baby's live appearance was
scheduled to go down. I called you and spoke to your
answering machine. Told you the date and time
for you to come and play pretend.
Sure enough, you were there to play the game. You were the first
one to hold her and the last one to do anything.
Four months after our baby's first appearance
Ran out of baby food and the baby had to learn how to eat ramen
noodles.
Came over to ask for help and you sat there and licked McDonalds
off each one of your fingers like it was sweet.. Told your bullfrog
of a
girlfriend that our baby wasn't yours. She was pissed off
when the paternity test was taped on her door.
Right along with the pictures of your pretend
performance at the hospital with those friends of yours.
I finally got to the point that I decided to stop
waiting on the wizard to give you a brain.
Woke up early one morning, opened the door, looked out at the
projects we were living in.
Made a promise that our baby wouldn't have to call
those bricks home anymore and if she did, it would only be while I

waited
on God to open another door. . .
Then I packed everything I could get into my Olds.
Buckled up my bundle of joy, and hit the road.
Stopping only to let your mother, who said she didn't blame
me for leaving, kiss my baby and say goodbye.
Leaving the audacity of your Stupid, Cheating Ass behind.

Why Ugly Men Cheat

Ugly men cheat
because they feel
like someone finally
gave them a chance so
they can't be as ugly as they
always thought they were.
And the person that has given them a
chance has started grooming them.
To make them easier on their eyes.
In other words, fixing them up.

The ugly man in transition sees other
women start looking and gets the big head
so they get the courage to talk to other women a try.
Disrespecting the one who originally
gave him a chance. Now he starts throwing lines.
Women he used to try to holla at
are seeing him in a new light.
They can't believe the man they
used to clown for being so ugly is
actually with someone and
is looking fine.
Now that he is someone else's
now they want to give him a try.

Cheating Man

He promised that he would
love me until the end of time
And I believed him
Even though there were places
he would go that I wouldn't know
and random numbers that would
pop up on his phone.
There were nights I would wait for him
to come home from his "friends"
house that knew how to braid.
Now you and I know,
he was over there getting laid.
Had some times when
his family would come
into town. I would ask to
meet them he'd frown and say
"Maybe the next time, I'll bring you around."
EVERY TIME
Come to find out, he was married,
and I was just *one* of the chicks he had on the side!
And then you have the one that cheated emotionally. Talking about,
"I didn't touch her! We never had sex!"
But them text say that all he needed
was just one more day.
Even though he didn't touch her
he crossed the line of no return.
That's why I say.

A cheating man will
always be a cheater no matter
how many women he hurts.

Proverbs From The Old

One day, there was a wedding getting ready
to begin at a church. An old man who
everyone took as the janitor, knocked
on the door of the groom's room
and asked if he could speak to him
for just a moment.
The Groom curiously obliged and pulled
out a chair for the elderly man.
He took a deep, raspy, breath and said.
Do the simple things she asks you to do
that you know she could do for herself,
when she asks you to, without complaint.
She knows that she can do the tasks herself,
and that she doesn't need you to.
But because you are her husband she
wants you to prove your love in small
increments at a time.
You are not always going to like what she
asks you to do or feel you have the time
but be careful with complaining or taking
your time in doing what she asks, for if
she does the tasks herself, she will begin
to doubt your love and wonder why
it's to you that she's married.
And when that sly fox who's been
watching all along see's that you're
not taking care of your husbandly
duties he will slip in and take care
of your tasks himself.

Proverbs Of The Old

Drawing your wife closer to him
In his bed she may not sleep,
but her heart he will keep.

All because he did all the
things she asked you to do
& more without complaint.

For the simplest way to please
your wife is just to do what she asks.
The same as she does for you.

Then the elderly man stood up and
put his hat, thanked the groom
For his time and left.

The groom's mother saw the man as he left
and asked her son what the man said to him.
As he told his mother what the elderly man
said tears welled in his mother's eyes.

Alarmed, the groom asks why she was upset.
She tells him that the old man was her father,
whom she hadn't seen in years.

Her mother had left him when she was only a child.
The reason why she left was because
he never did the things she asked

and she fell in love with
someone else.

Sins Forgiven, But Never Forgotten

I know you wonder if

I remember the times

you changed my life.

And I do.

But I refuse to let your sins

dictate the way I choose to

live although, I acknowledge

that your sin changed me.

Ironically your sin

added to my character.

I can discern when people

like you are in

my atmosphere.

It's like a deer being able

to sniff the air and know

When it's in danger.

Election

The people voting with skin like mine
for this Triple K members, will be the first ones strung up.
I wonder will that big, pearly white, cheesy ass smile still be on
their faces? If those green pieces of paper with
white dead faces will help them off that tree.
Will there be someone that screams out,
"No! This is wrong?!" Or will they watch
silently as the soul finds a new home?
It's as if we are watching a live version of
",Get Out."
We are screaming for these brainwashed
versions of our people to WAKE UP!!!!
But they don't hear a thing we say.
they are no longer one of us.
Their minds, their bodies,
Belong To Them.
Their souls we
can't touch.

How The School To Prison Pipeline Came To Be.

One day, a emergency meeting was called by the contributors of the Federal Prison System and law makers of this land we live in.
The meeting was called due to the low numbers that were counted all over the U.S. in the prisons.
The Speaker of the house stood to begin the meeting.
"We want to thank you all for coming to this meeting. We have a serious dilemma that needs to be handled with haste! "The attendees look at each other with perplexed expressions Wondering what could have happened.
"The count for black inmates in prisons has drastically dropped. And the count expected for black students from the schools has dropped too. At this rate, the trillions of dollars we've made off of modern day
slavery will be what has to be spent out to hire people at minimum wage to do the job we've been paying inmates pennies for. We have to figure out how this happened and fix this situation immediately!"
Someone from CPS raises their hand. "Well sir, we have had less calls from school personal and counselors reporting false claims of abuse. So now children have been respecting
adults and actually doing what they are supposed to in the classrooms.
Which limits the numbers in the reports we send to you."
Someone from the school system raises their hand.
" Sir, I have to say what cps just said is true. The tests you gave us to give the students in 3rd grade are actually being

worked on and all though they may not be high scores, the scores are not low enough to make a prediction on how many prisons cells need to be built. Along with that, the Black kids have actually been finding out about their history and it's giving them a sense of pride we've not seen in a very long time. Which we believe is adding to the dilemma."

How The School To Prison Pipeline Came To Be.

Someone from the Judicial System raises their hand.
"Sir, because of the discipline at home and the respect in the schools there have been less crimes committed by juveniles. No out of control warrants taken out on children by their parents. And no diversion cases to be denied by the district attorney. Which means no black youth are being charged with felonies at young ages. Which normally give us the count for how many prison cells would need to be making. Another thing is when we have tried to push the felonies some of the parents knew their rights and got lawyers too. So that their child's record wouldn't be affected."
The corporate tycoon that called the meeting began to pace and looked at everyone in the room with a stern face. "Very disappointing. People, we have got to do better!
Starting now!
Just Us, I mean *Justice System*, put in place laws so that any type of discipline done results in a report of child abuse whether it be right or wrong. If it's not reported, that school employee loses their job. This program will be a **Child *Production* Service** for *us*. But will still be called **Child Protection Services** throughout the U.S. "
If black students get in a fight, charge them both with assault.
I don't care who started the altercation. To cover up our plan, start a, "Diversion Program So it looks like we give a damn. But as soon as the case is submitted, have the district attorney deny it and have charges added to the black student's record. Making him a juvenile delinquent.

Tell the parents that they can have the charges expunged when they turn eighteen. But by then it will be to late. It won't mean anything. The damage will have already been completed. They will already been assimilated into the system. Add another charge for not going to school.
They won't realize they can go to jail for that too.
Let's call the part of this plan, "The School to Prison Pipeline."

How The School To Prison Pipeline Came To Be. (Continued)

If you follow these instructions, will have our inmate numbers back up in not time.

Now listen up and take notes. The following things I say is how we will execute our mission and get the most votes. Erase **EVERYTHING** that states black people invented **ANYTHING**. I don't care if it's the traffic light or air conditioning. They are not to know! It would give them hope!"

Get the Pharmaceutical Industry involved and get these kids doped up on drugs for ADD, ADHD, ,Depression, and Anxiety, instead of figuring out ways for them to deal what's bothering them. Infest the black neighborhoods with opioids like marijuana, heroin, crystal meth, and crack cocaine. With drugs in the blood lines that will speed up the need for drugs mentally. If the drugs are taken by blacks, lock them up. If they are white, call it an Opioid Epidemic.

Get liquor stores on each and every corner in the black areas of towns. For every church we need at least two or three liquor stores right next to each other. Make it cool to "Act a fool" You know them niggers work on, Monkey See, Monkey Do. And get those damn Black Panthers disbanded!!They will destroy this plan before it can be initiated!" The tycoon stands up and claps his hands.

"I think that's a great start! Any questions, ideas, or other demands?

Nothing else? Meeting adjourned. Let's go out and do everything we can to, "Make America Great Again". With the meeting adjourned, everyone stands to leave and sticks their white hoods in their pockets or up their sleeve. Happy with their directives, and a secure plan in mind. They raise their hands midair and say their closing phrase.

Ready to wreak havoc on Black lives that matter.
That's why society started all these rules. When we discipline our kids and teach them who they are, that keeps them from turning our future leaders into slaves they have to work for mere pennies a day in their prison systems they've planned for our seeds to stay.
Dear students I know you think this is a bedtime story
and you've gone to sleep.
It's time to WAKE UP, and be the great people we were created to be!

S.T.P.P

Let it be known that the
School To Prison Pipeline exists.

It's as real as the air you breathe.
Just as air is something you can't physically see,
the evidence is all around you.

STPP begins with a paper trail. Those that don't assimilate
have their incidents placed in their school records.

The defectors may have mental issues, some have ADD,
ADHD, they may have learning Disabilities, what some call BAD.

In a lot of cases the latter is usually the reason.
And real parents, the one that try, get CPS called
because they choose to discipline.

The kids know this so they use those three letters with reckless
abandon to get their way. Nowadays parents have no say.

So what do they do? They call the police on their kids too.
Go to the courthouse and get the beyond control warrant to
protect themselves from the life they gave birth to.
All the while falling into the plan of the school to prison system
too.

See the truth will never be told that this is the plan devised by the
slave owner for which your great grandfather 3x back was sold.

To keep the black family torn apart.
Mother from Daughter,
Father from Son

Knowing that because we would never
learn our history we would never realize
the damage that had been done.

The Bridge Burner & The Under Cover Boss

Young one, you asked,
did I have permission to tell you what to do.
I don't care if I do or not, but when
I say something to you face to face
It's so you won't say that I am
running and snitching on you.
You see not only is it the fact that,
I am a teacher that teaches your age,
but its also that I am a
Old School Adult an O.S.A.. That lives by the,
" R.Y.E.- Respect Your Elders," philosophy.
I don't care about a pay range, and I'm
not trying to be your friend.
And if you felt like I was trying
to tell you what to do,
in spite of me blatantly saying I'm not trying to,
then I feel sorry for you.
Because the job and that I was trying to hire you
for is the job you don't even realize you've already lost.
Ironically, I, was your undercover boss.
A bridge was being built
and you burnt it up before it could ever be completed.
Another thing you didn't know was that I am a poet and
I would be writing this poem about you.
Here's my last lesson to you if you haven't
caught on to the first one.
#NPOAP Never Piss Off A Poet.
Cause the next poem that poet writes,
will be all about you.
And child, if you were to read that poem,
you'll know what it means
to be cut without someone ever laying a hand.
It's not the words that a poet says,
but the words a poet write that hurt the most.

I'm a Thug

I teach classes so students can be better
off than me when they grow up
Cause I'm a Thug
I buy pencils, paper, Science Math and English supplies
from my own pocket
Cause I'm a Thug.
I make home visits and speak positivity to my students and their
families
Cause I'm a Thug.
I teach my students that they are capable of greatness.
No matter where or what they come from.
Cause I'm a Thug.
I teach my students that it is wrong to take what doesn't
belong to you and that it is called stealing
Cause I'm a Thug
I believe in kids who are told
they will never be anything in life.
Cause I'm a Thug
And if that makes me a thug
I'm cool with that
I'll be that Thug
So my kids
will have a great life
and be better than me and you
in all they do
Cause I'm a Thug.

Can You See?

*Oh say can you see
how the States came to be?*

*They brought us here as slaves.
To pick tobacco and their cotton.*

Built buildings, Raised Their Kids
While they still call us Niggers.
Raped, whipped and hung us
killing us for the fun
But we are the ones they call thugs
Act like they don't understand
When we speak against
what has been done to our
Mothers, Father, Daughters,
and our Sons.

Act like we should
forget the pain
forced upon us
their dollars to gain.

Strange fruit hanging from trees.
They were ancestors to me.

No matter how we try,
they will never see the light.
School to prison pipelines
Keeping our people locked inside.

*Oh say does our fists
raise to the
Red, Black, and Green!*

We stand for our Rights!
And forever we will fight!

He Doesn't Understand

My husband doesn't understand why

I stress if he's alright when he hasn't come back
30 or 40 minutes after he's gone to the store.

Why I stress about where he works and
the amount of White people he works for.

Why I didn't want him going to the bar
with his coworkers after the company dinner.

Why I feel like he's not paid enough
and feel like he should be getting paid more

It's because of the years of mistrust
that's grown for the people with white skin.

That has hung, shot and choked
people the same color of our own skin.

So when I call and ask where's he been when
he doesn't come home after a few minutes

It's not because I think he's cheating
I'm making sure he's still living.

The Phenomenon

It was the night before Christmas and all through the town
not a child was sleeping not one in any house.
All of the parents had gone to town to get Christmas toys
for their little girls and boys.
But what the children didn't know was that a town hall meeting had
been called that would steal all their Christmas joy, toys and all.
At the meeting there was a video that showed what the kids had been
doing wrong all year long. It was decided that the kids didn't deserve
to sing not even one, Christmas song. So the parents went back home
with visions in their heads of their children, whom they thought were
doing so good, being bad instead. On the way home the parents went
back down Memory Lane.
They thought of the time they were kids and remembered that
they would've never dared do the things that their kids had done.
They realized only then what kind of parents they had.
That instead of them trying to be their friends,
they were simply just, Mom and Dad.
So they began to do the same post haste. The kids were so surprised
when instead of Christmas toys they got the gift of Tough Love,
something they could not waste. When the children tried to say
something disrespectful to any adult, A strange phenomenon began to
happen all over the town
The children would black out and wake up on the floor.
With their heads, or their backsides feeling really sore.
The only thing out of place besides themselves would be
a single shoe laying near the door or a belt.
None of the kids knew what was happening to them all they knew
was that any time they were disrespectful the
phenomenon would happen even more!!!
Fast forward 12 months and Christmas has come again.
As is the norm the parents leave the house to go into town.
But this meeting was different.
This time the children were in attendance and were
awarded for all the good deeds they had done.
There were so many Thank You's, yes mam's, and yes sir's
The reporters nearly hit the floor!

They asked the parents what type of phenomenon was this that all of their children were so nice, and polite.
The parents looked at the reporters, smiled, and replied,
"There was no phenomenon at all.
It takes a whole village to raise just 1 child!!!
We were not their friends, we were parents to them all!!"

Sick

Comment on my post this morning: I have been sick for 8 years...
lol
My health insurance went up over $6000 during Obama administration.
My response to this comment was:
Hi, just seeing your post which answers the question I had about the text you sent to my phone. Obama Care was signed into effect in 2010. 2 years after Obama was voted into office. It wasn't until 2014 that people were fined for not having an insurance policy. I am sorry your insurance went up 6000.00 during the last 8 years, but I don't think the current "Administration" was the whole reason my dear. Also there are plenty of other reasons that I'm sick.
1. Someone that has openly shown what type of person they are would hurt rather than help people that are different than himself, has a very important position in the White House.
2. I'm sick because I have my child and my students asking are they going to be deported because of the person who sitting in the Oval Office.
3. I am sick because when people who were like the person that got voted in, my people were spit on, beat, were attacked by dogs, had fire hoses turned on them, and were lynched, all because of the color of their skin and because they felt that they deserved to be treated like a human beings. I am so scared that all of that may start happening again, in this land that's supposed to be so beautiful, united and free.
4.I'm sick because the person that has been elected President thinks its ok for hands to be placed on a black woman when she is in a place where she has every right to be. Even though she disagreed with the majority.

5. And I am sick because the person that is the President Elect can look down on women, make "locker room" comments about grabbing women in their private area, have multiple sexual harassment charges brought against him and still be elected. So if you are still reading this I hope you can see that my feelings about this situation are about more than the issue with insurance. I hope everything works out with your situation. I am still grateful for you helping me get my car and I will still tell people to come to you to get a car as I've been doing.

Sending Blessings Your Way, The Networking Queen. I got no response.

I Am A Woman

She rose earlier than the sun,
shook her husband awake,
went down the stairs, and began the task
they were supposed to do together.
When the task was complete, she started on
the other things that needed her attention.
Her husband asks,
"Why did you complete that task all alone?"
She turns to him and sweetly replies." I wanted you
to know that, I don't need you,
I want you.
I want you to do those manly things
like moving furniture, taking garbage out,
disciplining the kids,
changing the tires and the oil on the car,
along with making sweet love to me.
But I don't NEED you to.
Because I am a woman,
There is nothing that I can't do.".
Then the wife went back to
fixing the leak under the sink.

I Want A Prolific Experience

I want an experience for soulful people that
love the Art of Real Music and Poetry.
That's filled with people who are fine
with not being part of a popular
clique or the "In Crowd".
I want an experience with people who
sing their stress away even though they
were told they couldn't sing because
they don't sound like everyone else.
I want an Experience where
Poets who have poetry in their
hearts and thrown aside notebooks,
"Speak Their Peace".
In spite of being told that they are
not "Real" or Slam Poets by people
that feel like they have a name for
themselves. I want to go into a zone that's
supposed to be "Judgement Free"
and not pay to be judged.
I want to experience people that are "Closet" Poets,
Musicians, and Singers that have never introduced the
mic to their spirit, walk up to a mic and let their spirits free.
I want to experience people filled with soul who aren't into
gangsta' rap, killing the spirit, and blatantly disrespecting
themselves.
People who have a love for art and love true old school, back in
the day,
R&B, Neo-Soul, with a kiss of real Hip-Hop from years before
these
babies were born and know where their help comes from. So it's
no surprise when you hear a gospel song come from their lungs.
I want an experience that I can grow from.
That when I leave, I know my soul
has been fed from.

I, want a Prolific Experience.
The Prolific Experience is an production filled with
poetic and music performances
add to that Black art and soulful people.

Join our email list at prolificservices502.info and the Prolific Experience
Facebook group to find out about our upcoming events!

www.ingramcontent.com/pod-product-compliance
Lightning Source LLC
Chambersburg PA
CBHW071217160426
43196CB00012B/2332